SIDE-DRIFTING FOR STEELHEAD

JD RICHEY & FRED CONTAOI

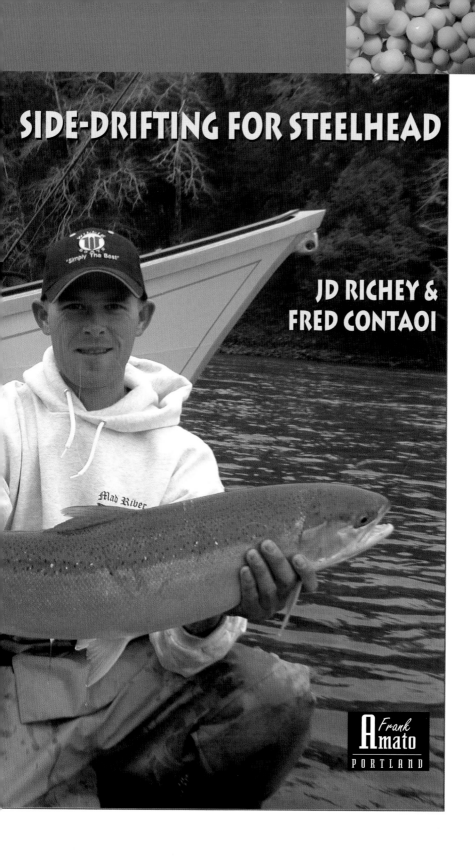

SIDE-DRIFTING FOR STEELHEAD

JD RICHEY &
FRED CONTAOI

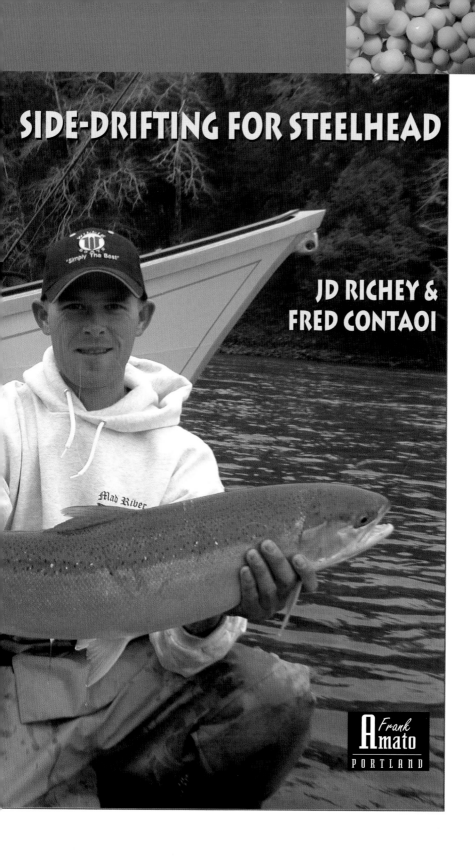

Frank
Amato
PORTLAND

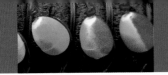

DEDICATION

To our parents, who taught us that there was actually a point to homework and studying, and to JD's wife Tamara, who kept us in line whenever we tried to get out of working on this project. Without her patience and encouragement, we probably would have missed our deadline by about 16 years.

Frank Amato Publications, Inc.

P.O. Box 82112, Portland, Oregon 97282

503•653•8108 • www.amatobooks.com

All photographs by the authors unless otherwise noted.

Illustrations by Tom Waters

Book & Cover Design: Kathy Johnson

Printed in Singapore

Softbound ISBN: 1-57188-350-9   UPC: 0-81127-00184-2

1 3 5 7 9 10 8 6 4 2

CONTENTS

Perfect side-drifting conditions on Northern California's Smith River. John Klar works his "dudes" through a very fishy-looking flat.

PREFACE

When Nick Amato, editor of *Salmon Trout Steelheader*, first suggested the concept of doing a book on side-drifting, we were at once excited and stumped. We were eager to be a part of something that had never been done, yet the task was daunting. After all, you can tell a person the basic principles of side-drifting in about 20 words—put on some good bait, use just enough lead to get down to the bottom, cast out and start drifting—so how the heck does one fill an entire book?

When we started peeling back the layers, however, it became immediately apparent that we'd need a series of books to adequately cover all the subtleties and nuances of side-drifting. At that point, our concerns shifted and we started brainstorming ways to condense such a broad subject into one volume and have it make sense. We pondered the question over greasy coffee shop breakfasts, in boats between bites and over cold beer in countless riverside taverns. Somewhere along the line, the answer finally came: keep everything as simple as possible and stick to the basics.

We've tried to keep everything as easy to follow as possible and have designed this book to get the beginner started down the path to becoming an effective side-drifter. If you're just starting out, this should give you everything you need to get your toes wet. Just remember that you also need to put in a lot of on-the-water time and be patient. You're going to get the hang of this but it won't happen overnight.

In putting this project together, we've drawn upon our experiences as full-time fishing guides and have also picked the brains of several other excellent guides and anglers. On that note, we'd sincerely like to thank people such as Nick Amato, Clancy Holt, Khevin Mellegers, Kevin Brock, John Klar, Brett Brown, Woody Wood, Gill McKean, Justin Gyger, Matt Kinne and Ron DeNardi for their help.

—JD Richey
Fred Contaoi
June 2004

INTRODUCTION

Before we can dive into the complex and sometimes thorny subject of side-drifting and how to do it, we first need a formal definition. The problem lies in the fact that the term "side-drifting" means a lot of things to a lot of different people. An angler fishing out of a 17-foot open-tiller jet sled on the wide and flat Cowlitz River clearly fishes differently than a driftboater working a smaller, boulder-rich stream like the Clackamas. Yet both consider what they're doing to be side-drifting. And it doesn't stop there. On steelhead rivers throughout the Pacific Northwest, California, British Columbia, Alaska, Idaho and the Great Lakes, there are about as many ways to describe side-drifting as there are anglers practicing it.

So, the bottom line here is side-drifting cannot be classified as a specific way to fish, but rather as a family of techniques. Included in the family are three similar, yet quite unique methods of catching steelhead: freedrifting, side gliding and boondogging. Let us explain…

Freedrifting: This is a technique mainly done from jet boats in which the lines are fished at a 30- to 45-degree angle upstream and away from the boat. Freedrifting is well-suited for larger streams with smooth cobble beds. Because the sinkers constantly tap the bottom when freedrifting, your baits can be fished at a controlled rate, which makes it a particularly attractive method in high, pushy and off-colored water. It will also produce in low and clear conditions provided you have enough room to keep the boat off the fish. From humble beginnings on the Lower Sacramento in the 1950s, freedrifting is now widely employed on countless steelhead streams—the queen of which is Washington State's Cowlitz River.

Side Gliding: Most commonly performed on clear-flowing rivers with snaggy bottoms, side gliding allows you to present baits to steelhead quickly and naturally with minimal bottom contact by keeping the lines slightly downstream of the boat. Most gliders fish from driftboats, but sleds can get in on the action as well. It's especially deadly in low and clear conditions, but gliding will produce even in moderately high water as long as there's a reasonable amount of visibility. Northern California's Smith River and Southern Oregon's Chetco are two hotbeds of side gliding activity, though it's also found its way to the upper Rogue, the Olympic Peninsula and tributaries of the Skeena system in British Columbia.

Boondogging: It's pretty simple, turn the boat broadside to the current, cast directly upstream and then drag the baits downriver at the speed of the current. Boondogging may

Regardless of technique, all side-drifters hope to end up in this position—a big wild steelie in hand. Guide Craig Bell is about to release this jumbo wild buck.

be the easiest form of side-drifting to master, but that doesn't mean it's any less effective. Best on big water or smaller rivers that have some color, this technique allows you to cover lots of ground in a short amount of time and is suitable for both jet sleds and drift-boats. Boondogging probably started on the Skagit River sometime in the 1940's and is now popular on streams like the South Fork Eel, Navarro, Snake, Klamath, Feather and some of the larger Great Lakes tributaries.

With those definitions in mind, we can now move on to the how-to section of this book. Realize that there is no one "right" way to do any of these techniques and every-body's got a slightly different approach to them. The following chapters are simply designed to help you grasp the fundamentals of side-drifting and to give you a strong foundation from which to build.

Each of the three techniques has its own chapter in which we'll cover concepts and tactics, followed by a chapter for each that will go over all the basic gear you'll need. We've also added some special tips and tricks we've learned from guides and anglers we've fished with along the way. When it is all said and done, you should be well on the road to becoming a proficient freedrifter, side glider and boondogger.

1
CHAPTER

SIDE GLIDING

As is often the case with fishing, pinpointing the exact origin of a technique is difficult. Usually, if a method's been around for awhile, its beginnings are clouded by a colorful veil of local legend, myth and wives' tales. That's certainly the case with side gliding. We can't tell you where or when it became a popular method for catching steelhead, but it was likely born of necessity on some steep, boulder-strewn river where the rocks have an insatiable appetite for lead—perhaps California's Smith River or the North Umqua in Oregon.

The Wright Brothers of side gliding probably developed the early versions of this technique to help keep tackle costs down. Somewhere along the way, however, they undoubtedly realized that, in addition to losing fewer sinkers with their new style of fishing, they also caught more steelhead—a lot more.

Side-gliders preparing for the first drift of the day.

Side-gliders showing good form—the lines are parallel and slightly downstream of the boat and their rods are at the proper angle.

The basic principle of side gliding is to minimize bottom contact by getting a bait/sinker to "glide" just off the bottom rather than drag along it. This is accomplished by keeping the lines slightly ahead of the boat and the use of lighter weights. An offering that has only intermittent contact with the riverbed (ideally, the sinker will graze the bottom every two or three seconds) will hang up much less often and will also drift in a very natural-looking fashion.

Kevin Pohley battles an early March native that bit a side-glided nightcrawler on California's American River.

Side gliding is a technique that requires both bait and boat to be moving swiftly downstream, which means it works best when the water has a reasonable amount of clarity and the fish can spot the bait from a distance. It really shines during low/clear conditions but will still produce when the water's a little pushy. Gliding is not, however, well suited for high, muddy water when the fish are tucked tight to the banks or when the water's extremely cold and the fish are lethargic.

Gliding from a Driftboat

Side gliding is most commonly practiced from a driftboat, though jet boaters will find it equally effective. We'll cover both styles, beginning with drifters.

Setting up for the Drift

To get a better grasp of basics, let's take a look at hypothetical situation in which you're the oarsman and you have two buddies up front:

There's a fishy-looking run against the left hand bank (looking downstream) that you want to fish. First, you need to position the boat about 40 to 70 feet out towards the center of the stream, so you won't drift over the water you plan to cast to. Have both fishermen put their baits on in advance and instruct them to flip their bails and get ready to cast. Being prepared is a major factor in this game because the lines need to hit the water within a second or two of each other to keep them drifting at the same speed. In that regard, side gliding is a team sport—especially when you have more than two lines in the water at the same time.

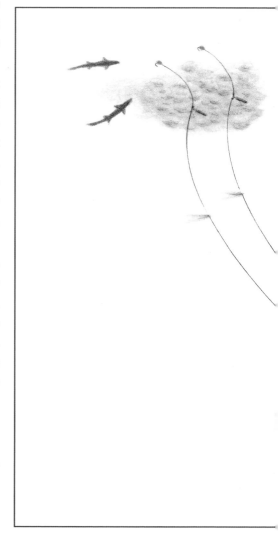

The Cast

Good casts form the foundation on which a productive day of side gliding is built. Without properly placed lines, getting a sweet drift is extremely difficult, so success really begins with the cast. When everybody is "cocked and loaded," the next step is to push on the oars to build some downstream momentum. If the casts are made while the boat is holding against the current, the lines will sweep too quickly downstream and won't touch the bottom. Once you've got a head of steam going, have the first angler throw his line straight out (perpendicular to the boat). As soon as his line hits the water, he should click the bail over (by hand to save wear and tear on the reel) and reel a couple times to take the slack out of the line. At that instant, the second cast should be hitting the water just upstream of the first. Angler number two should try to match the distance of the other cast, that way the lines will drift as close to the same speed as possible.

SIDE GLIDING

Most side-gliders fish their baits ahead of the boat. Some, however, fish directly off the side of the boat, especially in heavy, rocky water.

CURRENT

© Tom Waters

TOM WATERS

JD Richey releases a chrome steelie that ate a glided bait in Oregon's Chetco River.

If one cast goes too far and hits some slow water near the bank and the other hits the swifter current near the middle of the channel, you won't get a good drift. What usually happens is the lines will cross and the one in the slow water will quickly start angling upstream of the boat, while the one that's in the current will speed downstream of your position. It's impossible to properly work two lines that are angling away from one another, so have everybody reel up and cast again. You'll know you have a good drift going when both lines are parallel to each other once they're down near the bottom. Despite your best efforts, however, there will be times when one line will overtake the other. If the angle of the two lines isn't significantly different, the two anglers can simply switch rods to keep the drift going.

Before we move on, a word about casting order: In a traditional driftboat, where both passengers sit side-by-side up front, there's no hard and fast rule to determine who casts

first. Some guides like to have the angler in the left seat cast first when fishing a left-hand spot and vise-versa. Others do it the other way around—on right hand spots, the left-sider throws first and the angler in the right seat casts to the left. Try it both ways and find the one that works best for you.

We do it a little differently than most. Our driftboats (20-footers) are rigged with open floor plans and movable seats. With this configuration, we'll line up our clients, single file, down the centerline and have them cast in order, beginning with the rod in the bow and then moving aft. With the big boat and open floor, it's quite easy to fish four lines this way. With that many baits in the water, we can carve a pretty wide swath through a run and cover each spot more thoroughly.

When gliding, follow your line with your rod tip as it swings through the drift.

The Drift

With all the lines now in the water, you'll want to pitch the bow of the boat slightly towards the drift. This allows your crew to face their lines and also gives you the ability

Gliding really produces in clear-water conditions, and small baits are often one of the keys to success. The small foam ball behind the roe is a soft drift bobber (this one's a Fish Pill) that gives the bait buoyancy and color.

to pull away from the lines as necessary to keep them tight. As the oarsman, your job is to keep the lines in the optimum position, which is slightly ahead of the boat—just a bit less than 45 degrees. If you've got the right amount of weight on, your sinkers will be running anywhere from just in front of where your oar hits the water to a bit behind (there will be somewhat of a bow in your line between the point it where enters the water and your sinker). The current pushing on the bow

Before it goes back home, this green-eyed beauty from Oregon's Trask River poses for the camera. Steep and rocky, the Trask is a dynamite gliding stream.

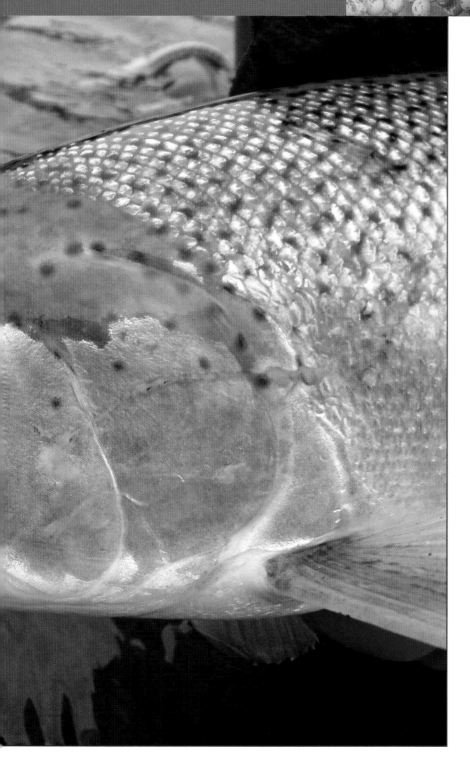

Dale Hutchins nets a crazy steelhead.

helps to lift and glide your weights over the rocks, just be sure that you get casual bottom contact so you know that your baits are in the strike zone. Again, if your sinker is tapping the rocks every two or three seconds, you're in business.

Having the lines downstream of your position also helps you, as the rower, see them and keep track of how and where everybody's drifting. You can, however, get too much of a good thing. If the lines get too far ahead of the boat, the sinkers will get swept up off the bottom and your bait will no longer be in "the zone." In that case, you're going to have to push on the oars to catch back up. Other times, you may notice the lines angling back upstream, which is caused by the boat traveling faster than the weights. To remedy the situation, try slowing the boat down by pulling back on the oars and/or switch to lighter sinkers.

It is also very important to keep your lines tight. In some situations, your sinkers will have a tendency to start "pulling" in towards the boat, which results in slack line. Without tension, it's difficult to feel the bottom and strikes become almost impossible to detect. By

pulling the boat away from the lines, you can keep them taught.

The Bite

Deciphering what's a bite from the tap-tap of your sinker as it occasionally skims the bottom is one of the toughest aspects of any form of side-drifting, especially if you're new to the

When you hook up, it's not a bad idea to pull over, get out of the boat and fight the fish from shore. That way you won't have to bypass any good water.

game. At first, "rock bites" feel very similar to fish grabs, but, as you practice, you'll notice that when a living critter picks up your offering, it's an entirely different sensation. No two bites are exactly alike, but in a textbook take, your sinker will stop bouncing and you'll get a light flutter on the rod tip. Of course, you'll sometimes get the no-doubt, rip the rod from your grip, suicidal slam, usually as your baits start to swing out at the end of a drift but those are not the norm when gliding.

While roe is the most popular bait for gliders, pink plastic worms can be deadly at times.

WILLIE BOATS

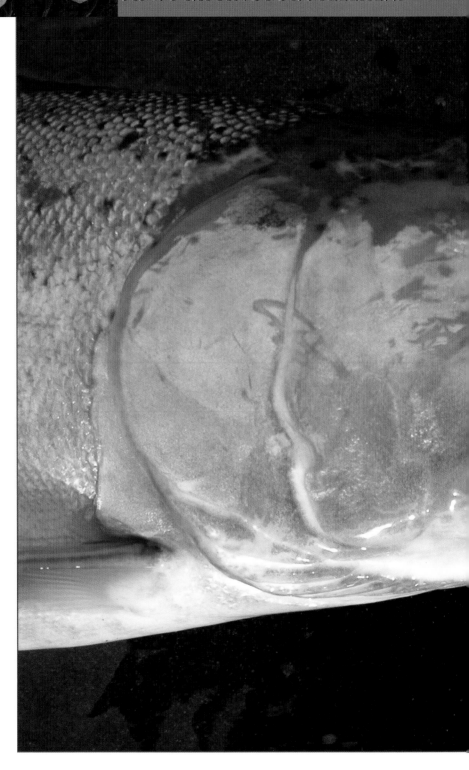

This Olympic Peninsula native couldn't resist a thumbnail-sized cluster of eggs spiced up with some pink and orange yarn.

Rafts and pontoon boats can help you get into those hard-to-reach spots.

Once you've determined that what you're feeling is indeed a bite, it's time to set the hook. Try to picture what's going on under the surface and you'll see why. In most cases, your bait should be drifting out ahead (downstream) of your sinker. When a steelhead grabs your offering, you may not feel anything until the sinker bounces downstream of its position and pulls the line tight against the fish. In those critical few nanoseconds, a steelie can mouth the bait and reject it before you have a clue that anything's happened. So when you do detect a bite, the fish has usually had your offering in its mouth for what, in this situation, amounts to an eternity and every second you hesitate decreases your odds of a solid hookset.

Rainbow trout are also suckers for glided baits. Kristen Edwards fished with JD Richey on the American River for this fat "bow" that ate a drifted crawler.

Since side gliding often takes place on rocky rivers, safety needs to be your greatest concern. Keep your boat properly balanced and always point the bow downstream. Get her sideways in something like this and you're in trouble!

Another thing that you can do, as oarsman, to help ensure the success of your partners is to carefully watch their rod tips. A trained eye is often more adept at detecting the faint nibblings of a steelhead than is the hand. Through the course of a steelhead season, we probably see 95 percent of the bites our clients get before they ever feel them.

Driftboat Safety

Over the years we've seen quite a few lazy knuckleheads in driftboats dragging anchors or buckets full of rocks behind them. This is usually an attempt to slow their boats down or to avoid rowing so that the guy in the oarsmen's seat can fish with the anglers up front. Whatever the reason, dragging an anchor is, in a word, incredibly idiotic. Okay that's two words, but you get the idea. There are just too many things that could go wrong, if the pick gets wedged in the rocks in heavy current, the boat can get pulled to the bottom like a giant baitdiver. Also, a 30- or 40-pound chunk of lead pulled through spawning redds does the fish no favors and, from a fishing standpoint, the consistent clanging of an anchor along the rocks is a big turn-off for steelhead.

Gliding from a Jetboat

Side gliding isn't solely the domain of driftboaters. Anglers fishing out of power boats can use the same principles illustrated above and catch plenty of fish. There are a few key differences to consider, however.

Boat Orientation & Safety

The biggest difference is boat orientation. When gliding out of a sled, you'll be drifting backwards downstream with the bow pointed upriver (as opposed to the other way around for driftboats). That means you have to pay very close attention to where you're going. As the driver, your most important job is to scan the water downstream of your position regularly and make sure the path is clear. Jet sleds have big, square transoms (and, often, kicker motors hanging off of them) that don't slide over stationary logs, rocks and gravel bars very well. Hit something solid and all kinds of bad things can happen.

Fred Contaoi made the perfect cast under a logjam while gliding on a Skeena River tributary and hooked this 22-pound wild buck.

Most side gliding is done from driftboats with 2 to 4 anglers aboard though jet boaters can also do well with this technique.

Just keep in mind that things happen very quickly and when you least expect it on moving water, especially when you get involved with watching rod tips, netting fish, tying leaders and rebating hooks. Don't let a great day of fishing end in tragedy.

Boat Control

While it is possible to catch fish while side gliding with your big motor, you'll find that your success rate will climb significantly if you use a kicker instead. Kicker motors are very quiet and don't displace much water, so you won't spook as many fish when using them. They also afford you much more fine control of your drift and presentation. Big pumps aren't exactly known as being highly maneuverable at slow speeds.

A skilled oarsman such as Kevin Brock always keeps his angler's line in the correct position.

2
CHAPTER

GEARING UP FOR SIDE GLIDING

T he first step in becoming a skilled side glider is to make sure you're properly outfitted. Due to its nature, this technique demands very specific tackle from the rod to the hook and all points between. In this chapter, we'll cover everything you'll need to make sure you get off on the right foot.

Though there was a sealion working the hole, this chrome Russian River hen couldn't lay off a side-glided egg cluster/Quickie combination fished by the Three Shady Amigos—Fred Contaoi, Justin Gyger and Gill McKean (left to right).

Matching Gear

Before we get started, it's important to point out that, regardless of which rods, reels, lines, sinkers and terminal gear you use, you need to make sure all the outfits you'll have in the water at one time are identical. Side gliding is all about getting the proper drift and very subtle differences in tackle can change the way a particular rig fishes. For that reason, we

always set our clients up with matching gear. To better illustrate this concept, let's take a look at the following hypothetical situation:

Okay, you're side gliding with three of your best fishing amigos in a jet sled. You're on the kicker motor, sitting this drift out. You've got the boat in position and instruct the boys to cast. Unfortunately, all your buddies brought their own gear. For sinkers, one's got a chunk of 3/16-inch lead as long as ball-point pen, another's using a Slinky stuffed with eight pieces of size .210 buckshot and the third dude is throwing a 1/4-ounce Bouncing Betty.

Shortly after the sinkers hit the water, you see the lines all tracking at different speeds. The heavy pencil lead is dragging way upstream and directly behind the boat, while the Slinky is about amidships and the Betty has swung so far downstream that it's no longer in contact with the bottom. You remember that having all your lines parallel is the key here and it's quite obvious that this drift isn't working out too well. So, you instruct the guys to reel up and all switch to the same size and style of weight. That should take care of the problem, right? Well...

This Michigan hatchery steelhead couldn't resist a pink worm glided along the edge of a logjam.

Slinkies and Sploosh Balls are the two main weighting styles used by side-gliders. These are both 1/2-ouncers.

They cast again, and though everybody's using the exact same weights, the lines still won't stay together. Closer inspection of their gear reveals the problem. Friend No. 1 is using heavy baitcasting outfit spooled up with 17-pound mono, while Friend No. 2 is fishing a 10-foot noodle stick with 8-pound fluorocarbon and your third compadre is rigged up with a 7-foot medium-action spinning outfit and 8-pound braid.

Because of its thickness, the 17-pound mono has more surface area to catch the current and thus gets pushed downstream at a rapid clip and leaves the other two lines in the dust. Though the two other guys are using the same test line (8-pound), the fluorocarbon has a greater diameter and drifts more quickly than the braid, which is about the same size as 2-pound mono.

Khevin Mellegers nets a lively steelhead on Oregon's Chetco River.

It doesn't seem like that big a deal, but line diameter has a huge impact on what speed your gear drifts through a run and that's again why it's so important to have everybody using matching gear. And since synchronized casting is a must in this game, it's good to have all your anglers using the same rods and reels. Plus, when guiding, we do a lot of tip watching and it's a lot easier to detect strikes when all the rods have the same action.

Rods

In general, most side gliders fish with spinning gear because it's easy to cast with, especially when beginners are involved. When choosing a rod for gliding, first be sure that it has enough backbone to handle the size steelhead you may encounter. Then, consider the characteristics of the rivers you fish.

Side gliding is much more effective when everybody on the boat is using matching outfits—everything should be the same: rods, reels, lines, leaders, sinkers and hooks.

On rocky streams where snags are a common problem, you're going to need a rod that combines stout backbone with a quick tip. One that fits the bill nicely is G. Loomis' 7-foot, 9-inch HSR 930—which is, quite possibly the most widely-used gliding rod on the West Coast. This rod's a lot shorter than most conventional steelhead sticks, but the reduced length makes it easy to handle in a boat, especially if you have to fish a lot of days with the rain top up. The HSR 930's stiff tip doesn't have a lot of flex to it, which helps keep sinkers from falling into snaggy crevices on the bottom as you drift. It's also got plenty of power to bury hooks and turn steelies that are hell bent on relieving you of all your line.

When fishing less grabby waters where you don't need quite as much pop, you can use rods with slightly softer tips like G. Loomis' HSR 900, Lamiglas' RR 76 MTS, Shimano's CSC-76PML or St Croix's 9'6" Avid AS96MLF2.

As far as casting sticks go, you're going to want to go a little longer for castability's sake, rods like G. Loomis' STR 1025C and STR 1086C and Shimano's CSC-86MH are great in waters where you need a lot of lifting power, while the G. Loomis STR 1024C and Lamiglas' X86LC Summer Run are dandy rods to use in waters where the fish are smaller and snags aren't a big issue.

Reels

Picking a spinning reel for side gliding is fairly simple. Basically, what you're looking for is a reel with a quality (front) drag system and a spool capable of holding 150 to 200 yards of 10- to 12-pound-test line. Shimano's Stradic and Symetre in the 2500 and 4000 sizes are nice, as are Penn's new Slammer reels in the 360 and 460 sizes.

We've got to admit, we're pretty partial to Shimano when it comes to baitcasting reels. For side-gliding with light weights, you can't go wrong with a 200-series Curado Super Free or Calais, and if you don't mind dropping some cash to step up to the big leagues, the Calcutta TE in the 100 or 200 sizes is about as sweet as it gets. Having said that, however, there are lots of quality reels out on the market and, for the money, Abu Garcia's 5500 C3 Ambassadeur's are great workhorses.

Fluorescent line shows up well against dark backgrounds, making it easier to keep track of. It shows up well under water, too, so you need to use clear leader material to avoid spooking the fish.

Line

When choosing a line for side gliding, look for one that casts well (with as little "memory" as possible), has a thin diameter and the durability to withstand frequent encounters with rocks, submerged logs, boat chines and big fish. Ten-pound Maxima Ultragreen has been the staple for legions of gliders for years and continues to be a favorite today despite the recent introduction of many other quality lines. P-Line's CX Premium in the 12-pound size is also a good bet as are Yo-Zuri's Hybrid, Suffix's DNA and Berkley Big Game.

Line Color

The color of the line is another factor to consider. When you're gliding, it's important to be able to see where all the lines are in relation to one another, which is often a difficult task during low-light periods or when fishing against a dark background. Squinting all day to see clear or drab lines can seriously tax your vision, so many anglers have made the switch to fluorescent blue, pink, yellow or green lines to give their eyes a break.

Except in super low and clear water, we've found that fish don't seem to mind at all, fluorescent line—which was a big concern when we first started using it. However, if you're having trouble with the concept of using laser beam-colored line, run a 5- to 10-foot section of fluorocarbon between your terminal gear and your running line.

Rubber Plunk 'N Dunk sinkers (Sploosh Balls) aren't as dense as lead and have a wider profile—both properties that make them glide effortlessly along the bottom. This one's attached to the line via a hard tie.

Braided Line

Though the majority of gliders still use mono, there's a solid case to be made for fishing with braided line. Braid features a combination of appealing traits that no monofilament can match. Being extremely soft and limp and containing no "memory," braided line casts like a dream. It's more resistant to twisting and won't come off in coils if you overfill your spool. Braid also has an extremely small diameter (30-pound test has the diameter of 8-pound mono) that cuts through the water with ease and resists being pushed by the current. The small diameter also allows you to put more line on a spool, which is particularly useful when fishing waters known to harbor jumbo steelhead.

Another advantage to braid is it's nearly bullet proof (in fact, some companies make it out of Kevlar, which is the same stuff that goes into bullet-proof vests). A hooked fish can wrap you around a stump or an oar or drag the line across the boat's chine and braid will usually hold. In short, it gives you a lot of confidence when you've hooked the steelie of a lifetime.

In general, you don't use very large baits when side gliding.

Braid takes some getting used to, however, and that's probably why some anglers have yet to jump on the bandwagon. This type of line has no stretch in it, so you have to learn to tone down your hook sets or risk popping the leader. You also get much-improved sensitivity with braid and dealing with the added "feel" takes a little getting used-to. It doesn't take long, though, to realize that strikes are much more obvious with this stuff.

When using braid (Power Pro and Tuf Line XP are two excellent brands), we don't tie it directly to our terminal gear. Instead, we'll run a section of Stren fluorocarbon between the braid and the swivel. The best way to connect the braided line to the fluorocarbon is with a loop-to-loop triple surgeon's knot. Be sure to make your fluorocarbon "pre-leader" just long enough that the knot can't be reeled down into the spool—otherwise, you'll have some casting problems.

Leaders

The length of your leader will depend largely on water clarity: in dark, murky water, use a shorter one and go longer when the river's clear. In dirty water, we run a 2- to 3-footer and then bump the length to 4 to 6 feet when the river's clear. Leaders should have a breaking strength that's about two pounds lighter than the mainline. That way, when your hook gets snagged on the bottom you can break off just the leader and not the entire rig.

Over the past few years, we've switched exclusively to fluorocarbon as a leader material. Due to its ability to closely match the refractive index of water, fluorocarbon is virtually invisible when submerged. It has very little memory, low stretch and is extremely abrasion-resistant. The one drawback to this type of leader material is it has a very sticky coating that makes knot-tying a little tricky. Just be sure to wet your line (or grease it up with something like Smelly Jelly) before cinching a knot down and you shouldn't have any problems.

There are several quality brands of fluorocarbon on the market today, including Seaguar's Carbon Pro, P-Line's CFX and Stren. Before purchasing a package, make sure the line is 100% fluorocarbon and not simply "fluorocarbon coated."

Weights

Considering the fact that one of the main objectives of side gliding (in addition to hooking fish) is to keep from losing a lot of terminal gear, pencil lead was abandoned on snag-filled rivers as soon as the Slinky arrived on the scene in the 1980's. Anglers quickly discovered that the new flexible sinkers were able to snake their way out of rocky nooks and crannies extremely well—and it's been a tackle box staple ever since. Pencil lead is extremely heavy and also has a "sticky" nature to it that causes it to really cling to the surface of rocks, whereas the parachute cord that encases a Slinky's buck shot slides over cobble with ease, allowing gliders to get a better presentation and fewer snags.

Long, slim sinkers made from .210-gauge shot are preferred for fishing grabby bottoms while magnum .250 shot is the choice for big, heavy water when you have to get down in a hurry.

Sploosh Balls

In addition to Slinkies, we also like to have a good supply of Plunk-N-Dunk sinkers on hand when gliding. At first glance these weights (nick-named "sploosh balls" for the sound they make when they hit the water) resemble Luhr-Jensen's Bouncing Betty—they're black plastic balls with a barrel swivel embedded in the top. However, Plunk-N-Dunks are much larger and made of a more

Sploosh Balls sometimes have trouble getting down deep but that problem can be easily fixed by drilling a hole in the bottom of the sinker and filling it with buckshot or a length of pencil lead.

It's a good idea to keep a large selection of sinkers handy so that you can be prepared for any water conditions you may encounter.

dense synthetic material. They are virtually snag free and glide beautifully along the bottom and are particularly useful in long, slow runs and shallow tailouts where other sinkers would lose momentum and hang up. The wide profile and relatively light body weight of a sploosh ball allows it to go where other sinkers can't.

But there are a few inherent problems with Plunk-N-Dunks. First of all, it takes some practice to get the feel for the way they drift. When fished on a sliding rig, they have a tendency to "roll" up the line towards the boat. And since they're plastic, it also takes longer for these sinkers to get down near the bottom so you need to set up for a drift a little earlier than you normally would. In instances where the sploosh rig just isn't getting down, we'll do a little aftermarket upgrading by adding some lead to them. You can do this a few different ways:

One method involves drilling out the bottom of the ball with a 3/16-inch bit and inserting a section of 3/16 pencil lead into the hole (just be sure all your lead pieces are the same length). Or, instead of pencil lead add 2 to 4 buckshot to the hole. The third and least aesthetically pleasing way to beef up your Slinkies is to go with the very okie, yet effective

"bean and frank" rig which involves fastening a 3- or 4-shot Slinky to the snap swivel that the ball is attached to. You won't win any style points with this one, but it does work!

Attaching Weight

Sinkers can be attached to the mainline via a "hard tie" or on a slider. With a hard tie, you simply run a snap swivel to the end of your main line, clip your weight to the snap and then knot a leader to the bottom eye of the swivel. To rig a slider, run the business end of your line through the barrel end of a No. 7-10 black snap swivel and then through a clear 1mm plastic bead. Tie a No. 7-9 black Rosco barrel swivel to the end of the main line and attach your leader to the other end. The sinker is attached to the snap swivel so it can slide up and down the line. Though a little more complicated, the sliding rig has some advantages:

First, when a fish runs into a submerged tree and the sinker gets caught in the branches, it can continue to run and pull line without immediately breaking the line. Secondly, sinkers like Plunk-N-Dunks have quite a lot of mass to them. When a fish jumps and

Slinkies rigged as a slider (L) and on a hard tie (R). To make the line easier to see, we used fluorescent pink to represent the mainline and yellow for the leader.

shakes its head in mid air, it can throw your weight around, which may result in the fish using that leverage to toss the hook.

Hooks

Catching steelhead isn't always easy. In fact, if you polled a random group of steelheaders, most would tell you that any day you get a fish or two to the boat is a win. Sure, there are those magical days when you hook 8 or 10 fish, but the reality of the situation is you're fishing for a few bites on most trips to the river. When that bite you worked so

A skein of perfect eggs—a side-glider's dream.

hard for finally occurs, you're going to want to have a quality hook stuffed inside your bait. Yes, the best hooks cost quite a bite more, but you gain so much by using them.

When you're getting picked clean by smolts, squawfish and trout, spawn sacks will prolong the life of your eggs.

They're usually stronger, lighter and sharper than their cheaper counterparts—all of which are qualities that can make a huge difference in your success rate.

In low and clear situations, when tiny baits are necessary, we'll use No. 4 or No. 2 octopus-style hooks and then bump up to sizes 1 to 2/0 as the water gets some color to it.

Baitholders

While octopus-style hooks work well for holding baits like eggs and shrimp they are not the best choice when you're using threaded nightcrawlers or plastic worms. When gliding "garden hackle" or pink plastic, we use a lot of size No. 2 or 4 baitholder hooks (again, Gamakatsu is a good

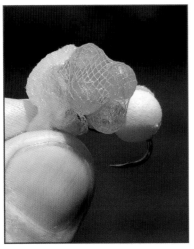

choice). The barbs on the backside of the shank help to hold the worm in place and keep it from bunching up on your hook. Baitholders are also the hook of choice when fishing with crickets.

Baits

Roe

Side gliders employ a wide variety of baits when pursuing steelhead but freshly cured roe is the favorite by a large margin. Packed with loads of protein and oil, a cluster of eggs is like a Power Bar to steelhead and is something they often have a tough time resisting. Everybody's got a secret cure they like to use on their eggs, but that's a subject worthy of many more pages than we have here, so we're not going to get into it. Instead, read Scott Haugen's in-depth treatment of the topic in *Egg Cures: Proven Recipes and Techniques,* which is also available through Frank Amato Publications.

The size of the bait cluster you use depends largely on the clarity of the water. In murky conditions, use a glob of eggs that ranges from nickel to quarter size. When

One-stop shopping: pre-cut egg clusters and foam BFDs, together, make for quick rebaiting.

Nightcrawlers are deadly steelhead baits, particularly for summer and fall-run fish.

visibility increases, drop down to the size of a dime (or even smaller when a river is low and clear and being heavily pressured).

We will sometimes use Contaoi's Battle Eggs, Glo Bugs, Jensen Eggs or Gooey Bobs in lieu of roe when there are lots of bait-stealing smolts in the river or on waters that are governed by bait bans.

Alternative Baits

There are times when steelhead just won't hit eggs. Usually, this happens when a river gets pounded by a lot of anglers and the fish simply get tired of seeing the same stuff

There are times when pink plastic worms will outfish anything on the river.

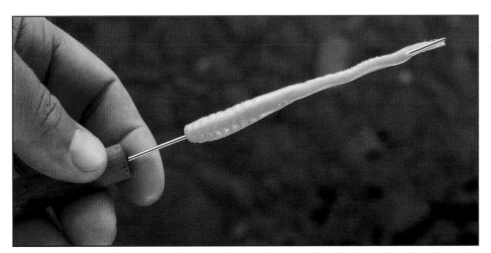

Plastic worms and nightcrawlers can be easily rigged with the help of a threader tool.

drifting past their faces all day long. That's when it pays to have a backup bait on hand so you can show the steelies something they haven't seen. Sand shrimp, cocktail shrimp and crawdad tails can sometimes be just the ticket to get stale fish to eat again. Pink plastic worms are also deadly at times—especially on late-running natives—and nightcrawlers and crickets are good choices when fishing for fish like summer steelhead that spend several months in fresh water.

Drift Bobbers

Drift bobbers serve two important purposes: First, they give your bait some buoyancy, which helps to keep it up out of the rocks and up where the fish can see it. Also, they add a splash of color to your offering which enables fish to more easily locate it. For decades, Corkies,

In waters with bait bans, side-glided synthetic egg patterns and nymphs can be very effective.

Cheaters and Spin-N-Glos were the standard bobbers used by side gliders, but in recent years small, fluorescent soft-foam balls, known simply as "puffballs," have become the staple for this type of fishing.

As far as we can tell, Northern California guide Rich Mossholder, is the father of the puffball (we like to call him Puff Daddy, but hear he prefers "P-Diddy" these days) and his Rivers West Outfitters' Puffballs were what everybody on the Smith and Chetco rivers used for years. Since then, several other companies have jumped into the game and now there are many brands to chose from, including Quickies, Fish Pills and Thunder Balls to name a few. Since there are so many people calling foam balls so many different names, we're going to try to avoid confusion by referring to them all as "BFDs" (bait-flotation devices) in this discussion.

BFDs come in a wide assortment of fishy colors and sizes. In general, we use light pink in low, clear water and then switch to fluorescent pink, glow pink or orange when the water has some color to it. In stained or murky conditions, bright orange, chartreuse or fluorescent red are the colors of choice.

Most side-gliders now use soft-foam drift bobbers sometimes called "puffballs" or BFDs (bait flotation devices).

Fred Contaoi holds up a gorgeous native hen for Harland Hendricks that hit eggs glided through a particularly snaggy section of the Trinity River.

Unlike Corkies, which have pre-drilled holes through which you thread your leader, you simply "skin" the edge of a BFD with the hook point and then slide it up the shank so that it butts right up against your egg cluster. They're a lot softer that the old-style drift bobbers, so when a fish bites down, it's less likely to reject your bait. Also, a BFD will break off your hook when you set up on a fish, leaving your hook gap free of obstructions.

BFDs are also much less expensive than other style of drift bobbers, yet another trait that endears them to anglers.

Yarn

You always hear that it's a good idea to run a strand of yarn through your egg loop because it can get caught up in the teeth of a steelhead, affording you a little extra time to set the hook. Whether or not that's really true is debatable, but there's no denying the fact that adding some yarn to your offering isn't going to hurt—just ask steelheaders in British Columbia who catch a ton of fish on straight "wool" on streams where bait is not allowed.

Most gliders shy away from yarn when the water is clear and use it only when flows are up and turbid. In darker water, go with some contrasting colors like bright orange and red and then use lighter colors like champagne pink when you've got some decent visibility.

3
CHAPTER

FREEDRIFTING

When Clancy Holt first visited the Cowlitz River in Washington State over twenty years ago, he wasn't looking to start a steelhead fishing revolution…but that's exactly what happened. With his old Wooldridge inboard sled in tow, he was simply on an exploratory trip, checking out places to potentially re-locate his blossoming guide business. The Cowlitz was intriguing because it offered better year-round fishing opportunities than did his home stream, the Sacramento River, on which it was hard to book trips during the winter months.

After making the long drive up monotonously-straight Interstate 5 from Northern California to the Cowlitz, Clancy did something extraordinary—something too few of us do when we get to new water—he kept the boat on the trailer and just watched and learned how all the other boats fished and interacted with one another. For two weeks he took in the scene from shore and, when he finally dropped his sled into the river, Clancy felt that

Guide Clancy Holt freedrifting the Cowlitz River in Washington State. Though it's been well over 20 years since he first popularized this technique, it's still the main way to drift fish for steelhead from a power boat. Here Clancy fishes with Nick Amato and Fred Contaoi.

Brett Brown with a freedrifted hatchery doe from Washington State.

he understood the protocol for fishing the busy river without ruffling the feathers of the locals. He was also pretty sure he had a better way to catch steelhead than they did. Though he didn't know it as it was happening, the moment that Clancy backed the big Wooldridge into the Cowlitz for the first time was an immensely significant event that would forever change the face of steelhead fishing.

Back then, most steelheaders in boats either drift-fished with eggs on anchor or pulled plugs, but Clancy was anxious to try something that he'd helped pioneer on the Sacramento many years before. "When we first started fishing for trout on the Sacramento in the mid to late 1950s, we would drop the anchor above the fish and then back-bounce eggs down into them," says Clancy. "But we eventually figured out that we could cover a lot more water if we drifted. So, me and a number of other guys in Redding started out boondogging and then we slowly refined it over time to get the baits

Fred Contaoi admires a freedrifted Washington steelhead after a nifty netting job by Matt Kinne.

drifting free, off to the side of the boat instead of dragging behind it. It really worked out for us and pretty soon drifting eggs and nightcrawlers was the main way we fished for rainbows and steelhead."

When Clancy made his first few passes with his Sacramento River freedrifting technique, the Cowlitz locals looked at him like he was stark-raving mad. Some even pitied the poor greenhorn. After all, not only was he fishing in a very unconventional manner, but he was also using spinning tackle—a sure indication, they figured, that Clancy was an

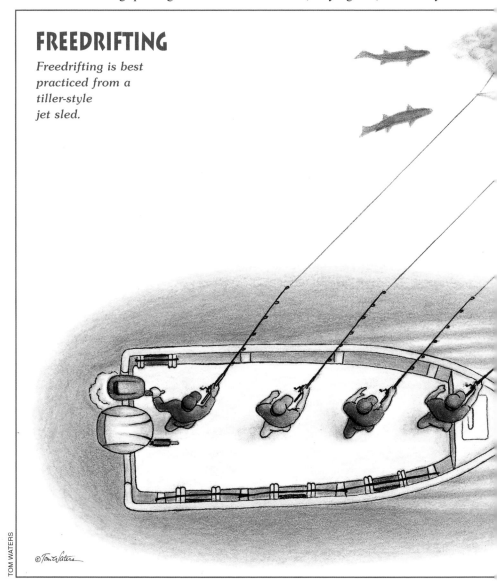

FREEDRIFTING

Freedrifting is best practiced from a tiller-style jet sled.

amateur. But the rookie from Northern California quickly put on a serious steelhead-catching clinic that left the river regulars blinking in disbelief, almost as if their brains couldn't register what their eyes were seeing. "It wasn't long before all those guides were ringing my phone, trying to figure out what I was doing," Clancy says. "Those fish just hadn't seen bait presented like that before and it totally changed the way they fished up in the Northwest."

Rather than suffer a daily beating at the hands of Clancy, the Cowlitz locals promptly

CURRENT

shifted over to drifting, and the rest, as they say, is history. Now, freedrifting is the only way to go on the Cowlitz and is regularly practiced on countless streams in the Pacific Northwest, Alaska, California, B.C. and larger Great Lakes drainages.

The genesis of freedrifting was spawned by the desire to cover as much water as possible and that's still the main reason it's so popular and effective today. And since it's normally done from a power boat, you can make as many passes as you need through a particular run. A boat also enables you to stay on top of schools of moving fish, and affords you the luxury of using light tackle.

Now, let's take a look at the basic concepts of this technique. In general, freedrifting is best practiced from an open tiller-style jet sled in which two to six anglers (depending on the size of the boat) can be lined up in a row down the centerline. When fishing, the bow is always pointed upstream and casts are made slightly up and across. With the lines in the water and the sinkers ticking the

bottom, the pilot keeps the boat drifting—with a kicker or electric motor— downstream at a rate that's usually a little slower than the current's speed. For the sake of better visualization, here's another hypothetical situation in which you and two buddies are fishing:

Setting up for the Drift

As usual, you're again stuck driving the boat in this little scenario. But, the good news here is that being the person on the tiller means you get first cast—and first water—all day. Anyway, there's a beautiful slot against the left-hand bank (looking upstream) that you just know has some fish in it. It's about 50 yards long, has a moderate current and is uniformly 4 1/2 feet deep through its entire length.

First, motor to the top of the slot, sticking as close to the right bank as you can afford to go—that way, you won't run over the fish to which you're about to cast. When you get to a point upstream of the run, kill the big outboard and fire up the kicker. With the bow pointed upriver, motor into a position that leaves you 20 to 60 feet abreast of the good water—get close when the water's up and discolored and stay off it more during low, clear conditions. Make sure your two friends are in a single-file line, baited up, facing the same

In a jetboat you can scale down your gear and really enjoy the battle.

Freedrifting out of a jet sled gives you the ability to fish a run as many times as you like. You can also stay on top of moving fish easily.

direction and are ready to cast. The casting order should go stern to bow, (though some like the reverse order) so you get to make the first toss.

The Cast

Back off the throttle and let the boat start to slip downstream and then cast at about a 45-degree angle upstream as close to the left bank as you dare. Then, instruct the guy in the middle of the boat to do the same. He should try to duplicate the angle of your cast and have his sinker land upstream of yours to avoid crossed lines. With line number two now in the water, your pal in the bow needs to toss his rig a little upstream of the second caster's.

Before we continue, let's briefly examine the plight of the bow caster. Of course, the big downside to being the guy in the front of the boat is your bait is always last in line to reach

JD Richey revives a British Columbia steelhead he hooked while freedrifting a spawn sack, or as the Canadians say an "egg bag."

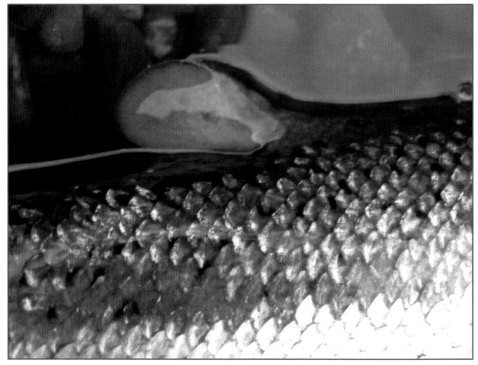

The adipose fin is intact, meaning this steelhead is wild and should be immediately released—even if the law allows retention of natives.

the fish. You also have to wait for everybody to cast and if somebody ahead of you flubs their toss and angles it too far upstream, you won't have much room with which to work. The advantage to bringing up the rear, however, is that you're free to "wildcat" cast at will. If your gear slides out of the main slot, you can reel up and re-cast without getting in the way of anybody. And should a sweet-looking spot materialize on the opposite side of the boat, you can make a quick toss in that direction—again, without upsetting the group's drift.

The Drift

In a perfect world, the lines will be evenly spaced and parallel to one another as the drift begins. As the driver, you're in charge of keeping them drifting properly with subtle bumps of the throttle (both forward and reverse). If the boat's slipping too quickly down-stream, the lines will start creeping back towards you and will eventually end up dragging directly upstream of the bow. Go too slowly and they will swing downriver of your position and out of the zone. Ideally, you want the lines to angle slightly upstream of the boat.

One main advantage to keeping the lines all running somewhat up and away from the sled is that you'll keep them tight. When freedrifting, a tight line will give you a better feel for bites and the bottom and you'll also get more positive hook sets. Also, as the driver, you'll naturally be facing the lines, which makes keeping tabs on how everybody's drifting an easy task. Without exception, there will be times each day when the lines cross. Sometimes you can get things straightened out by jockeying with the throttle, but there will also be instances when the lines will overlap regardless of what you do. That's when fishing out of an open sled really shines—when one guy's line overtakes another, the two anglers can easily swap places and keep the drift going.

Your sinkers should be in regular contact with the bottom, tap-tap-tapping all the way through the drift. Under normal conditions, the right amount of weight will keep you on, but not pounding, the bottom. In stained or off-colored water, however, you should add extra weight to slow the presentation down so that the fish have a longer look at it.

The Bite

As is the case with all other forms of side-drifting, determining bites from bottom taps when freedrifting is the big challenge for beginners. Occasionally, a steelhead hell-bent on suicide will destroy your bait and all but yank the rod from your grip, but it's not always

Fred Contaoi displays a fresh Klamath River native for Erin Lehnhard.

such a slam dunk. A lot depends on how fast the bait is traveling and from which direction the fish intercepts it. You'll get a pretty obvious take when a fish heading upstream stops a swiftly-moving bait. On the other hand, steelies will sometimes turn and follow a bait downriver and the bite is a lot more difficult to read when you, the bait and the fish are all moving in the same direction. Water temperature will also influence the way the fish bite. In cold water, bites are often sluggish and barely distinguishable from the bottom. When you've got warm-water conditions, however, you'll get much more enthusiastic and aggressive takes.

Each bite is going to be different, but generally speaking when a steelhead stops your bait, the sinker will stop ticking the bottom and you'll get a squishy feeling in your rod tip as it starts to load up. If that's followed by a throbbing sensation, the fish has your bait in its mouth and is either aggressively chewing on it or shaking its head in an attempt to spit the hook. From start to finish, you've got no more than about two to three seconds to figure out what's happening and set the hook.

In an effort to help our clients gain a better understanding of what a bite feels like, we'll have them look down into the water at the riverbed and ask them to visualize their sinkers bouncing along the cobble. If an angler can start to grasp what his/her weight is doing as it skips along rocks, bounces off boulders, falls over steep lips and bangs into wood, they'll be more confident to set the hook whole-heartedly when they do get bit. When steelheading, you work so hard for every bite and it's extremely deflating when

The lack of an adipose fin indicates this fish is of hatchery origin.

JD Richey with a B.C. steelie that hit a scaled-down freedrifted rig in low, clear water.

somebody misses a good take because of an unsure half-set. Getting a feel for what's bottom and what's not will also save lots of bait and increase your fishing time. It's a pretty simple equation: The less you set the hook on rock bites, the longer the bait lasts. The longer the bait stays on the hook, the greater the chance that a fish will see it.

Safety

Most freedrifting accidents take place when the skipper gets too involved with fishing or some other task and stops paying attention. As you drift stern-first down a river, rocks, deadheads and gravel bars pose a very real threat to your kicker's prop and lower unit and they can also potentially knock you in the drink or sink your boat if you hit them hard enough. Remember, partially-submerged objects are more difficult to spot from the upstream side and they can sneak up on you very quickly. Also watch out for stuff like log sweepers and low bridges. Drift under one of these obstructions and nothing good will come from the experience.

When you're fishing immediately above something hazardous like a big rapid, falls or logjam, be sure to stop your drift earlier than you normally would so you have a little extra time to get the kicker up and the big motor started. And speaking of getting the engine running, always keep your outboards in excellent running condition—your life could depend on it.

4
CHAPTER

GEARING UP FOR FREEDRIFTING

Freedrifting out of a jet sled is an extremely effective and efficient way to catch steelhead and it also affords you the luxury of using light tackle. With the boat, you can chase even the hottest steelhead down in relatively short order, so beefy rods and giant reels with deep spools aren't necessary. It is mandatory, however, that all your outfits match one another—just as they should when you're side gliding. Having everyone on your boat fishing with identical rods, reels, lines, leaders, hooks and sinkers simply enables you to get better, more predictable drifts.

When fighting big steelhead on light line, most freedrifters like the forgiving properties of long, soft rods.

In all but the clearest conditions, fluorescent line is the way to go when you're freedrifting. It's easy to see and allows you to always know where your line is.

Rods

Clancy Holt popularized the use of spinning gear for steelhead freedrifting over two decades ago and it's still the main way most anglers go today. In situations where light weights need to be delivered to distant targets, spinning tackle really shines. Plus, it's easier for novices to handle than backlash-prone conventional gear. If you have accomplished anglers aboard, however, there's no reason you can't fish effectively with baitcasters. For the sake of this discussion, we're going to stick with spinning outfits since that's what most people freedrift with.

In Washington State, where the world's largest concentration of freedrifters resides, G. Loomis' 9 1/2-foot STR 1141 spin stick is the standard. Extremely soft and rated for 4- to 8-pound test, the rod initially seems too light for the task, but you have to remember that you can scale way down when fishing out of a boat. The rod's length makes long leaders easier to cast and the soft tip gives the fish an extra second or two to chew on your bait before they feel any resistance. During a hook-up, the forgiving parabolic bend of the STR 1141 acts like a leader-protecting shock absorber and will also help you keep the line tight.

The only drawback to fishing with such a limber stick is that you won't have a lot of pop with which to free a sinker from the rocks should you get snagged.

Other good choices for freedrifting include the Lamiglas 9 1/2-foot EC 96 LLS and Rogue's SS 963S. If you'd like a little shorter stick, try the 9-foot CSS-90ML-2 in Shimano's Clarus series and the WS90LM2 by St. Croix in the same length. And for larger fish, check out G. Loomis' STR 1082S.

Reels

A freedrifting reel should have two key features: a smooth drag and instant anti-reverse. A quality drag system is essential for protecting light leaders and wearing down strong-willed fish. Instant anti-reverse keeps the play or "slop" out of your reel's crank which is a big help in both the hook-setting and fish-fighting processes. Another feature to consider in a reel is a long-stroke spool. You'll give up some line capacity for casting distance, but you don't need to store a ton of line when fishing from a boat.

There are lots of quality reels out there: Shimano's Stradic and Symetre in the 2500 series are excellent, and Okuma's Size 30 Inspira and Daiwa's SS 1600 are also worthwhile. In addition, Penn and Abu Garcia produce several serviceable models as well.

Fluorescent pink, green and yellow lines show up well against a dark background and are real eye-savers.

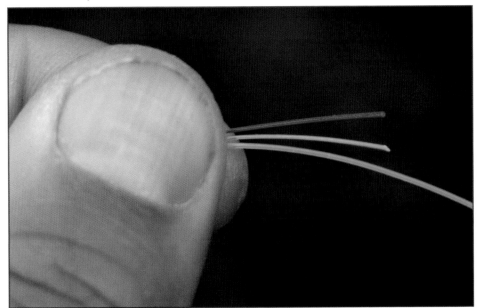

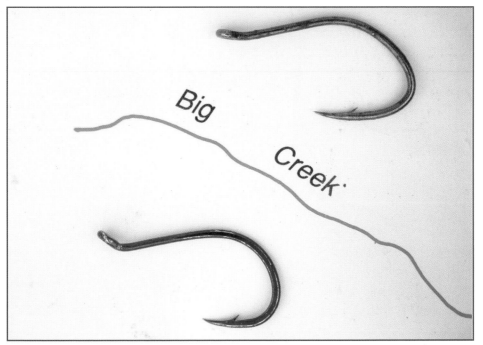

Gamakatsu's octopus bait hook (bottom) has long been the staple for freedrifters, but the VMC Vanadium and Mustad Ultra Point have been gaining popularity in recent seasons.

Line

Freedrifting lines need to be at once both soft and tough. Because you'll sometimes need to cast reasonably long distances, your line must be supple but it also should be durable enough to handle encounters with rocks, logs, tree limbs and boat chines.

Braided line fits the bill nicely as it's softer than mono and is virtually indestructible. When using long, flexible rods like those listed above, braid's lack of stretch will give you better hook-setting power and the small diameter means you'll be able to put more of it on your reel. Braid doesn't develop a "memory" like mono does, so it casts smoothly and comes off the spool straight, rather than in coils. Thirty-pound Power Pro is the overall best choice for freedrifting with braided line.

Braid isn't perfect, however, and it can be tough on both tackle and engines. It's so strong that you can sometimes snap a rod tip when you lean too hard into a fish or a snag. And it can also cause all sorts of problems if you suck some up into your jet's impeller or wrap your prop.

For those who feel more comfortable with mono, Izorline, Yo-Zuri, Suffix, Berkeley, P-Line and Maxima all offer castable, hard-wearing lines. To better be able to see and keep track of all the lines on your boat, consider using one that's fluorescent yellow, green, pink or blue in color. Twelve-pound test will work in most situations, but when you have to throw tiny weights in low and clear water, drop down to 10- or 8-pound mono.

Leaders

Unfortunately, snags are an unavoidable reality when you're freedrifting. Keep in steady contact with the bottom all day long and your lead is going to find its way into some unmovable underwater obstructions from time to time. With that in mind, you're going to want your leader to be lighter than your main line. That way, if your hook hangs up, you can break it off without losing

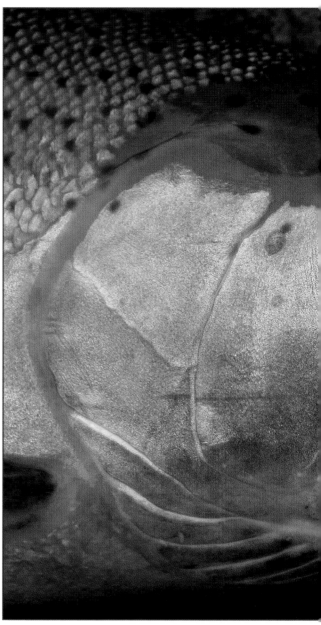

A Skykomish River buck that took freedrifted eggs.

the entire rig. When we're fishing with mono, we'll use leaders that have a 2- to 4-pound breaking strength lighter than the main line we're running. With braid, we'll run a section of 14- to 20-pound fluorocarbon "pre-leader" between the braid and the swivel and then

attach a lighter (8- to 12-pound) section of fluorocarbon to the swivel to serve as the actual leader.

Under normal conditions, a 5-foot leader made from 10-pound fluorocarbon is just

The Slinky on the bottom is rigged on a slider while the top one is hard-tied directly to the main line.

about right. In extremely clear water, we'll bump that length out to as much as 7 feet and go with 6- or 8-pound test. In murky conditions, however, a short leader works best and you can drop it down to 3 or 4 feet and increase the breaking strength to 12 or 14 pounds.

Weights

Freedrifters have two choices when it comes to weighting systems: pencil lead and

Tandem hook rigs—go large in high water and drop down in size when the flows are low (again, the green line is used for photographic purposes).

Slinkies. Pencil lead in the 3/16-diameter size is the overwhelming favorite because of its ability to get down in a hurry. It also transmits a clear "tap" up to the rod tip each time it bounces off a rock, while Slinkies give off a softer feel that can sometimes be mistaken for a bite.

Pencil lead is very grabby, however, and is most effective when used on bottoms that are relatively smooth and free of snags. If you're on a river with an uneven bottom and lots of big rocks, Slinkies are a much better choice, but don't use them in woody spots. In areas of heavy fishing pressure, where anglers lose lots of gear, pencil lead works better because Slinkies can easily get impaled by hooks caught in the rocks. Catch your Slinky on a derelict hook anchored to the bottom and you're probably going to lose your entire rig.

When attaching sinkers to your line, fasten smaller weights via a "hard-tie" and rig larger ones up as a sliding arrangement. See the weights section in the Side Gliding chapter for more on this subject.

You typically lose a lot of gear when freedrifting, so it's a good idea to have plenty of pre-tied leaders on board.

Hooks

Gamakatsu and Owner Super Needle Point octopus-style hooks in the No. 4 to 1/0 sizes are standard equipment in most freedrifters' tackle boxes, though VMC Vanadium (7356 BN) hooks have been gaining a following in recent years as well. The Vanadiums are sharp and nearly impossible to straighten out. They also feature a deeper bend that really seems to hold hooked fish in place. They run about 20 percent smaller than other brands so No. 2, 1 and 1/0 are the best choices for freedrifters.

When freedrifting, there are times when you'll want to switch from a single hook to a double-hook tandem rig with a Corky or Cheater sandwiched between the two. The two-hook setup will increase your bite-to-hookup ratio and will also help keep your bait from spinning as it drifts downstream. Fish have a hard time swallowing baits on double rigs, which will save your leader from rubbing across their teeth and it also makes releasing them unharmed much less of a challenge.

Baits

Most of the time, you can't beat freshly-cured salmon or steelhead roe for bait when freedrifting, but there are occasions when other baits will out-fish it. When the area you're

A good supply of Slinkies will help you adapt to ever-changing conditions.

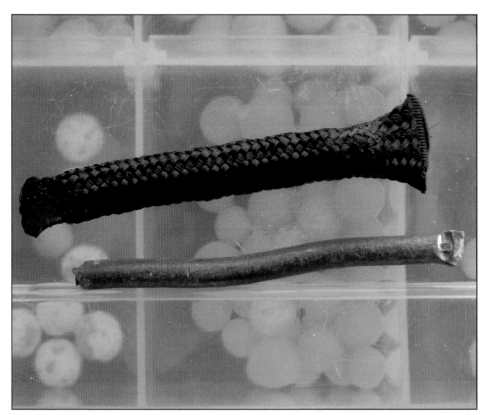

Pencil lead and Slinkies are the two weight styles most commonly used in freedrifting.

fishing is getting pounded by a bunch of other boats, give an alternative bait like cocktail or sand shrimp a shot. In waters that harbor aggressive late-running native steelhead, a pink plastic worm can be just the ticket and live nightcrawlers can work wonders on summer fish.

Driftbobbers

Most freedrifters aren't overly concerned with getting their baits to drift up off the bottom, but it certainly doesn't hurt to give them a little lift with the help of a driftbobber. Corkies and Cheaters are the most common driftbobbers, though Spin-N-Glos also have their moments. Use size-14 bobbers in light orange and pink shades in clear water and size 10 in brighter patterns like fluorescent red, orange and chartreuse when the water's dark or stained. If fishing gets tough, drop the bobber program entirely and fish a naked bait.

5
CHAPTER

BOONDOGGING

H ere's a fun little exercise to try sometime: go into a bar full of steelheaders and ask them to define boondogging. Like a match to dry tinder, you'll spark a heated discussion that will last into the wee hours, and when the smoke finally clears, you'll probably have just as many definitions as anglers seated at the bar. For some reason, there's a lot of ambiguity when it comes to boondogging in regard to what it actually is, where it started—and even how to spell it. So, we're going to set the record straight right here and now.

Let's take it from the top, beginning with the spelling of the word. Some insist it's spelled with an "l" as in "*boondoggling*," but take a peek at a dictionary and you'll see

Boondogging is a great way for driftboats and sleds to cover lots of water when the fish are spread out. This B.C. silverside was boondogged out of a long straightaway on the lower Skeena River.

When you drift over a school of steelhead, double-headers are not out of the question. This pair of frisky Feather River fall-run steelies went for roe and green Spin-N-Glos.

that to boondoggle is actually: *To take part in a wasteful or impractical project or activity.* Considering how many steelhead and salmon are caught with this technique every season, that definition is way off base, so let's leave boondoggling to the politicians. The other way you'll see the word written is *boondogging*, which is the proper spelling, we believe.

Now that the issue of spelling has been addressed, let's move on to the definition of boondogging. It seems that the term is tossed around rather loosely in steelhead and salmon fishing circles and anglers often use it interchangeably with freedrifting and side-drifting. In reality, however, you're boondogging only when you pitch the boat broadside to the current, cast straight upstream

JD Richey hooked this B.C. buck on boondogged roe. He jumped out onto the gravel bar to chase it while partner Fred Contaoi battled the other end of a double-header out of the driftboat.

and drift down the river with the lines bouncing along the bottom upstream of your position.

Though the exact origin of the name of this technique is unclear, by most accounts the first boondogglers were loggers riding rafts of timber down the Skagit River in Washington State. On the way downstream, some would cast lines off the upstream side of the logs and drag chunks of lead and drift bobbers along the bottom. The big log islands passing overhead often agitated the steelhead enough to put them into a biting mood and the loggers caught lots of them, so many in fact that the technique caught on with boaters. The term boondogging may have evolved from driftboaters who followed (dogged) the log booms and fished behind them—as in they "dogged the booms"—and somewhere along the line, the "m" in boom turned into an "n."

In any case, boondogging caught on in a big way and is now employed by thousands of steelhead and salmon anglers from Alaska's Kenai and Nushagak rivers to the Snake River in Idaho to the St. Joe's in Michigan to the Klamath, Sacramento and South Fork Eel rivers in Northern California and all points in between.

Boondogging is a great "searching" method with which you can cover lots of water in a relatively short amount of time. It's easy for beginners to pick up since precision casting isn't necessary, and guides love boondogging because they can run up to six rods at a time without major tangle issues—something

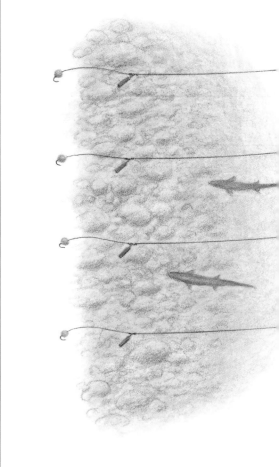

BOONDOGGING

Boondoggers drag their bait directly behind the boat.

that would be very tough to do when side gliding or free-drifting. Boondogging is most often preformed from jet sleds, but drift boaters can effectively fish this way as well.

Setting up for the Drift

Start by motoring upstream of a good-looking piece of holding water and, with the bow still pointed up river, hold in the current and take a look downstream for any potential hazards to navigation before you begin the drift. Also take a moment to try to predict where

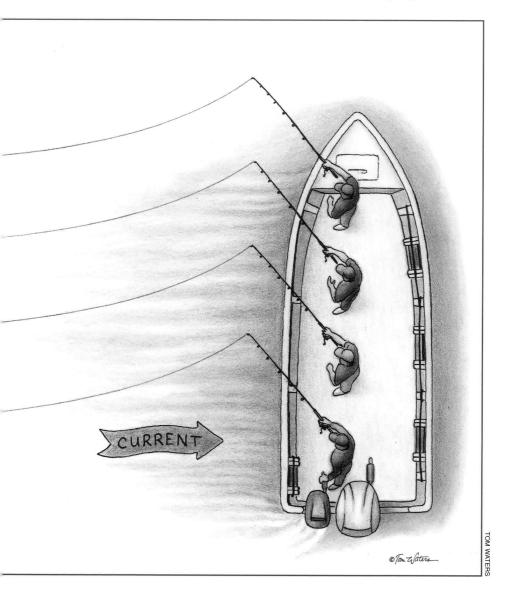

CURRENT

©Tom Waters

Boondogging Chetco River style.

A boondogged Central Valley chromer.

the current is going to lead you so you can get in position to take the best possible line down through the run. When you're ready to fish, kick the boat sideways to the current and start your downhill drift.

The Cast

As we noted earlier, casting is the easy part of this whole program. All casts should be made directly upstream and parallel to one another. How far you need to throw is governed by the water's depth, clarity and speed; in shallow or clear conditions, a long toss is necessary to get a little separation between the baits and bait. Casts can be shorter in slower or murky water, however. In general, go with the shortest possible casts in a given situation so that you have better control of the lines. Most of the time, you'll be tossing anywhere from 30 to 65 feet upstream.

We like to position out best caster in the middle of the boat so he/she can establish a "center lane" which the casters in the bow and stern can use as a guide. Once you have a good straight line running upstream, have the casters on either side try to match the distance and angle of the center line.

You can also simply drop your rig into the water on the upstream side of the boat and play out line until you feel the sweet spot where the sinker is getting to the bottom, but not pounding it.

The Drift

On paper, boondogging shouldn't work. First of all, being at the mercy of the current, you don't have any control of the tempo of your drift. Secondly, since the river's speed will be faster along the surface than down on the bottom, you end up dragging your rig downstream, sinker first. Imagine a steelhead sitting on a shallow flat…first a boat drifts directly overhead, then a chunk of lead, moving at Mach 3, hits it on the nose and finally, the trailing piece of bait comes into view. Theoretically, it's about as lame a presentation as there is, but somehow it works. Again, part of the technique's effectiveness lies in the fact that you can cover long stretches of water and put your offering in front of the maximum

Sometimes the best water isn't always easy to get to. JD Richey runs his 20-foot barge through some heavy water.

Sitting on his rod butt while working the oars, JD Richey just about lost his stick when this Northern California native hit his boondogged eggs.

number of fish. And, as the Skagit loggers found, stale fish will sometimes "wake up" and get grabby after a boat runs over the top of them.

To get the best possible drift when boondogging you need to use the right amount of lead. We run just enough weight to keep the bait tapping on the bottom—you'll know you've got the right amount on when the bait skims, but doesn't pound, the bottom and you have little or no bow in your line. Use too much lead and you'll get snagged more often, use too little and the lines will lift off the bottom and out of "the zone."

As captain, your job is to keep the vessel broadside to the current and the lines tracking straight through the best water. The key to keeping a good drift going is to stay ahead of the game. If you can anticipate how the current is going to push the boat, you can make slight corrections accordingly and stay on the fishy water longer. Wait until the current starts pushing you off course and you'll get behind the power curve, which leads to a lot of lousy drifts.

Some jet sledders still boondogg "old school style" with oars, but most now control their drifts with the help of kicker motors. Kickers are great because you actually get to fish while you drive—instead of driving while your buddies fish. From a guiding standpoint, the use of a motor frees us up to be better able to help clients with tangles, re-baiting and re-rigging.

In high water, steelhead can be spread out. Boondogging is a great way to locate pods of moving fish.

A bright 5-pounder out of the American River about to live to see another day.

The Bite

Boondogging, as they say, isn't rocket science. When you're blazing downstream at a high rate of speed, there are only two things that will interrupt your drift: snags and fish. At the point of initial contact, both feel similar in that your rod tip will load up. Snags will remain solid, while your tip will pump and feel spongy when you've got a fish. Another helpful clue to keep in mind is that a hooked fish will often "come with you" as the boat continues to drift downstream, while a snag will stay put. If the rod loads up and line doesn't fly off the reel, it's a fish. Since the boat moves so rapidly away from the fish in this

Most jetboaters boondogg with the help of a kicker motor, but some still prefer to do it the "old school" way with oars.

One advantage of the drifter, you can launch virtually anywhere that looks fishy.

technique, steelhead will regularly hook themselves—a big bonus when you've got rookies on board.

Boat Orientation and Safety

Without a doubt, the most important aspect of boondogglin' to consider is safety. It's inherently very dangerous to drift sideways down a river at a high rate of speed, with everybody facing upstream. Clip a rock or a partially submerged log and the sudden jolt can knock people into the water or even flip the boat. As skipper, you have to constantly scan the water downstream of your position as you go. When setting up for a drift, make note of potential trouble spots and orient the boat so that the bow (the stern in a drifter) points in the opposite direction, that way you have maximum thrust to push away from the hazard as you get closer to it.

A lot of boondoggers stand up while fishing and most have a tendency to creep towards the upstream gunwale. Have your guys stand on the center line of the boat, that way, if you hit something, they'd have a better chance of staying out of the water. Or better yet, run seats down that centerline and have everybody sit down.

6
CHAPTER

GEARING UP FOR BOONDOGGING

Boondogging is the least-sophisticated of all the techniques in the side-drifting family and your gear can be similarly basic. In previous chapters, we've stressed the importance of having everybody on the boat using the exact same outfits, from the rod to the hook and all points between, but boondogging is the exception to the rule. Assuming you have enough lead on, all your lines will generally drag behind the boat regardless of what kind of gear everybody's rigged up with. But, don't get us wrong here, having matching gear is still definitely the better way to go, but it's not as vital.

Rods

Spinning and casting gear are both well-suited for boondogging and what you decide to use really boils down to personal preference. Either way, your rod should feature a supple tip and plenty of backbone in the lower reaches. The soft tip section will allow a steelie to

Hard-tied pencil lead is the most commonly-used weighting system for boondogging.

Spinning or conventional gear works equally well for boondogging.

chew on your bait longer as you drift away from it and the backbone will give you the power to turn a hot fish.

For a spin stick, G. Loomis' 9-foot, 6-inch STR 1141, Lamiglas' EC 96 LLS, St. Croix's AS96MLF2 and Shimano's 9-foot CSS-90ML-2 are all excellent choices for boondogglin'. If you'd rather go the baitcasting route, try the G. Loomis 1143C or the Lamiglas X 96 LC.

Reels

Casting long distances is not a big part of boondogging so all you really need is something with a good drag and instant anti-reverse. There are lots of quality reels out there from which to choose, by the likes of Shimano, Daiwa, Penn, etc. The same holds true for bait-casters; pick one that's smooth, features anti-reverse and has a beefy drag system. Any of the ones mentioned in previous chapters will work just fine.

Line

On our own rods, we use a lot of braided line when dragging bait because we like the sensitivity it affords. However, beginners should start with mono because it has more stretch

Justin Gyger boondogged a spawn bag to entice this B.C. behemoth.

to it, which can buy you an extra second of time when a fish clamps down on your bait. Snags are easier to deal with when using mono as well.

Line takes a beating on the rocks and other assorted underwater hazards when you're boondogging, so it's a good idea to go with a brand that has an abrasion-resistant coating. Don't worry too much about picking a limp line because, again, casting is not a big deal here. Since all the fish you hook will be upstream of your position, you can use lighter line with this technique than any other, and 8- to 12-pound test will get you by in most cases.

Leaders

In the rods section of this chapter, you'll notice that most of the ones we suggested are all 9 or 9 1/2 feet in length. One of the main reasons for that is we normally use fairly long leaders when boondogglin'. The idea here is to put a little distance between the sinker and the bait. As noted earlier, your lead travels downstream ahead of the bait when you're boondogging which can occasionally spook a fish. With a long leader, the fish has the chance to recover from the shock of the lead and still have time to react to the offering. In dark or murky water, we'll go with 3- to 4-foot leaders and in clean water, we'll bump that length up to 5 to 7 feet.

To avoid breaking off entire rigs on snags, use leader that tests 2 to 4 pounds lighter than your main line.

Weights

Boondoggers have a couple of choices when it comes to weighting systems: pencil lead and slinky-style sinkers. Each has its merits and neither is perfect for all situations. Slinky weights glide a little better than straight lead, but they don't get down quite as quickly. They're great when fished over boulders and big rocks, but have a tendency to snag in wood. Pencil lead, on the other hand, gets down very quickly, but is a lot more grabby.

Hooks

Under most circumstances, we use single No. 4 or No. 2 Gamakatsu octopus-style hooks when dragging bait because they don't weigh much. The light weight allows us to add a driftbobber to our bait that will get it up off the bottom where a fish is more likely to notice it. Larger hooks have a bigger "bite" area to them but they also require the use of big bobbers to give them, enough lift to stay out of the rocks—bobbers so big they may actually repel fish.

Baits

All the baits you'd normally associate with drift fishing...crawlers, pink plastic worms, sand shrimp, crawdad tails, etc. work for boondogging, but roe is far and away the most popular and effective offering. Cured roe has a strong scent to it that fish can pick up even before they see it and its bright color helps it stand out against a drab background.

Drift Bobbers

Drift bobbers are extremely important for boondoggers in that they add color to the bait

In dark or stained water, dress your eggs up with a Spin-N-Glo (left) or a Wobble-Glo.

Slinky on a hard-tied rig.

Typical boondogging rig.

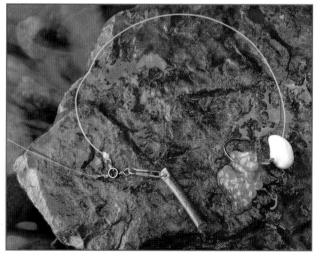

and also give it the buoyancy it needs to stay up in the strike zone. Under most circumstances, we use BFDs (puffballs), but there are times when No. 8 or 12 Spin-N-Glos will really turn the fish on. As a general rule of thumb, go with pinks and light oranges in clear water and fluorescent reds and oranges in darker water.

7
CHAPTER

BEYOND THE BASICS
ADVANCED TIPS & TRICKS

The real key to becoming an expert angler is to never quit learning. Pay close attention to what you're doing and try to understand why it works and, more importantly, why it doesn't. Also, make an effort to talk with other anglers as much as possible, everybody has their own perspective on how to do things and there's a lot to be gained by shooting the breeze with the guys at the boat ramp or in the parking lot.

Fred Contaoi scooping a British Columbia steelhead for Justin Gyger. The fish sucked up an egg bag filled with Pautzke's Balls O'Fire side-drifted under a float.

Fred Contaoi drifting some perfect strip-cast water.

Over the years, we've been fortunate enough to fish and talk shop with some of the best steelheaders on the continent, from whom we've acquired a deep vault of tidbits, tips and techniques that have helped us become more effective fishermen. We'd like to share a few of our favorites here:

Side-Floating

Fishing with floats has long been a popular and extremely productive way to catch steelhead, but it's mainly done by bank anglers or those fishing from anchored boats. A trip north of the border with Gill McKean and Justin Gyger of West Coast Fishing Adventures in Terrace, B.C., however, showed us that side-drifting with floats can be exceptionally deadly.

Eggs and a balsa slip float rigged for side-floating.

The technique is very much like side-gliding and freedrifting in that you toss your gear straight out or slightly upstream and then let it fish through the run as the boat slips downstream. The big key to successful side-floating is making sure you get a drag-free drift. If a belly develops in your line, it will pull the bobber and bait downstream at an unnatural pace, so you have to constantly mend the line like a fly-angler would.

A good way to understand the benefits of float fishing from a moving boat is to take a couple buddies fishing and have one freedrift or side-glide an egg cluster in a conventional fashion and have the other fish

By paying attention to all the subtleties of a river, you'll gain a better understanding of how steelhead behave under different conditions. Armed with that knowledge, you're sure to get more hook-ups.

eggs under a bobber. At the end of the day, you'll notice that the float guy spent a lot more time with his gear in the water. In shallow or slow spots through which sinkers cannot make it, floats will drift along with no problem. And since the bait stays suspended up off the bottom, snags are not as big a concern when fishing with a float. It's pretty simple: the longer your bait is in the water, the greater your chances of hooking up.

There are a million different bobber styles suitable for side-floating and you can hang a wide assortment of baits below them. In Canada, pink worms are popular with float anglers, as are Jensen Eggs, Gooey Bobs and wool (yarn). Along the West Coast, roe and marabou jigs are used most often, while spawn bags get the nod in the Great Lakes region.

Aluminum bait box/leader roller units are handy and help you maximize fishing time.

For years, bank fishing with flies under floats has been an extremely productive technique for us and our success rate climbed even higher when we started side-floating out of the boat. We normally suspend stonefly, caddis and mayfly nymphs and Glo Bugs under floats and hold them down with splitshot. The technique works well for winter fish in low, clear water and is absolutely lights-out when summer steelies are around.

Since we have limited space here, we're not going to dive too deeply into float-fishing tackle. For more information, check out Dave Vedder's book *Float Fishing For Steelhead* by Frank Amato Publications.

Rolls of pre-tied leaders strategically placed in the boat will limit the amount of downtime you have each trip.

Pitching for Steelhead

Small brushy streams often get overlooked by side-drifters because they're just too hard to fish. Casting can be an exercise in extreme frustration when there's lots of overhanging brush and trees and getting a good drift in tight quarters is usually next to impossible. However, solid populations of wild fish frequently exist in these under-fished waters, and Khevin Mellegers, an innovative guide and co-owner of Mad River Outfitters in Arcata, CA has figured out a way to get at them.

His technique is best described as bass fishing from a driftboat. Using a stripcasting outfit with a short 12- to 18-inch leader, he pre-measures just the right amount of line to

Pitching with a stripcast outfit is one of the best ways to present baits to steelhead in small, over-grown streams like this one in Southeast Alaska.

Steelhead don't come easy and everything you can do to learn more about them will pay off in the long run.

hit his spot and then makes a sidearm/underhand ("pitch") cast. If he correctly judges the distance, his line will straighten out and drop perfectly just short of the brush. If Mellegers sees that he's overshot the target, he can pinch the line with his left hand to stop it before it goes into the trees. With the precision casting ability that the stripcast outfit affords, he can fish tiny openings in cover unreachable with conventional tackle.

Once the bait is in the water, he'll bump his sinker along the bottom as if he were side-gliding or freedrifting. The big difference is the drifts are generally a lot shorter on small streams, so he has to pick up and re-cast a lot more often.

Mellegers makes his own custom stripcast rods out of 8 1/2- or 9-foot drift rod blanks. He likes heavy blanks rated for 10- to 17-pound test so he can handle big fish in small, snag-filled pools. For a handle, he uses a large, full-wells style cork and a 4- to 6-inch fighting butt. He's found that mono sticks to the rod blank when it gets wet, making casting a difficult proposition, so he uses small single-foot ceramic guides forward of the three lower stripping guides to keep the line and rod separated. For reels, Mellegers' favorite is a Fin-Nor 3:1 multiplier filled with 100 yards of 15- to 20-pound Maxima spooled over backing. He says that a No. 9 or 10 fly rod will also suffice for stripcasting.

On small waters, a low profile is important to avoid spooking the fish, so it's best to pitch for steelhead from downsized craft like pontoon boats and prams rather than high-sided drift-boats.

Speed Drifting

The speed that your baits drift along the bottom can make a huge difference in how many bites you get on a given day and guide John Klar, one of the most prolific side-gliders we know, feels that faster is better in most cases.

Under normal to medium-high conditions when the water has good visibility, Klar uses as little weight as possible so his baits fly downriver at a high rate of speed. The quick presentation is very natural-looking and also gives the fish a lot less time to scrutinize his offerings. In addi-

Vince Thompson used updated flow and temperature readings off the Internet to formulate his game plan for the day...which resulted in a sea-fresh native.

tion, Klar hangs up less frequently when he's using the lightest sinkers possible and that translates into more time spent fishing instead of re-rigging.

Klar's high-speed approach also allows him to cover a lot of water and get his baits in front of the maximum number of steelhead.

Side-Drifting Flatfish

When steelhead are getting pounded by boats in a particular stretch of water and go off the bite, you can sometimes turn them back on by showing them a little something different. One of our favorite things to throw at the fish under such circumstances is F7 Flatfish.

We drift these little plugs pretty much like you would a chunk of bait: A Slinky or pen-

Side-drifting with small plugs like F7 Flatfish can put fish in the boat when all other baits fail.

cil lead for weight, a 3- to 4-foot leader and then the lure. F7's are very well suited to boondogging and freedrifting and you can be pretty sure that nobody else on the river will be fishing with them. Don't expect a typical plug take-down when a steelhead picks up a drifted Flatfish, however. You'd think the fish would murder them like they do Hot Shots and Wiggle Warts, but the take is really a lot more like a bait bite—soft and spongy.

This technique actually works well in most conditions, even when there isn't a lot of other angler pressure. It is also worth trying when big native steelhead are present. These fish are generally much more aggressive than their hatchery-reared cousins and will angrily chomp down on a plug when nothing else is working. Just be sure to replace the stock hooks with a size No. 2 or 4 Gamakatsu siwash hook attached via a quality barrel swivel—or run the risk of potentially losing the fish of a lifetime.

Silver, gold, chartreuse and fluorescent red are all good basic colors to have onboard though F7 Flatfish come in a huge assortment of patterns, so don't be afraid to experiment.

Poor Man's Driftboat

On every river, there are a few fish-holding spots that are not conducive to drifting with a boat. Usually, there's a log, rock or shallow spot in the boat's path that makes these spots unfishable. Rather than bypassing such honey holes, you may be able to freedrift them from the shore.

When fishing "poor man's driftboat style," you better be ready to run if you hook a hot fish. Here's JD Richey in pursuit of an Eel River bruiser.

Freedrifting from the bank ("Poor Man's Driftboat" as Khevin Mellegers calls it), was originally brought to our attention by Nick Amato, editor of *Salmon Trout Steelheader* magazine, and is exactly as it sounds. You make a cast slightly up and across as if you were in a boat and then start walking with the bait downstream. At the end of the run, you reel in, hike back upstream and cast again. It's a laborious process but you can cover the water in a hurry and get a much better drift than you would if you were standing in a stationary position.

It works particularly well on wide gravel bars just above tidewater areas, where the fish are often spread out and is also nicely

When steelhead are holding tight behind structure like boulders, logjams and bridge supports, flogging is the best way to get at them.

suited to the lower reaches of heavily-logged streams which are typically wide and flat.

Both Amato and Mellegers like to get groups of anglers involved in Poor Man's Driftboating and say that it's a fun way to fish because everybody gets a chance at the best water, not just the guy who happens to be standing in the right spot. They also like it because they have a lot more control of the speed of the drift when walking as opposed to rowing. Just be sure to look down as you go, it's easy to trip when you're watching your rod tip and not paying attention to where your feet are going.

Flogging

Contrary to how it sounds, flogging is not some sort of medieval torture tactic. It's actually a great way to get baits into hard-to-reach runs that most anglers bypass. Brett Brown, guide and owner of Alaska King Salmon Adventures, taught us this technique while we did some fun fishing with him on his home water in Washington State.

Flogging is the solution to those pesky spots on rivers that are deep and short. Say there's a boulder that has a perfect 5-foot-deep pocket behind it that's only 10 or 15 feet long. With a conventional side-drift approach, your sinkers will never get down in time before the slot tails out. To handle such a spot, put on a very large chunk of pencil lead and then set the boat up just off to the side of the spot, no more than 10 or 15 feet away. You want to stay close so you can keep better control of your line. Toss the lead into the head of the run, if you have enough on, it will get down immediately and start bouncing.

The great thing about flogging is you get to fish water that bankies and other boaters have all missed. Be the first bait through one of these short spots and you've got a good chance of getting bit.

The Dialed-In Boat

In the winter of 2003, we had the pleasure of fishing with legendary guide Clancy Holt on the Cowlitz River in Washington State. In his 40-plus years of guiding, Holt has had a hand in some extremely important advancements in river fishing, including freedrifting and sardine-wrapped plugs for salmon fishing. He also helped to popularize the use of open-tiller-controlled jet sleds for salmon and steelhead fishing. These days, Holt is as particular as ever about his boats and the one we fished out of was a spectacular exhibit of how a dialed-in boat can improved your fishing efficiency.

The rig we rode in was a enormous 25-foot, 5-inch-long Alumaweld open sled (powered by a mammoth Mercury 225 HP four-stroke outboard) with an impressive 82-inch

Guide Clancy Holt's 25-foot sled is a superb example of a dialed-in rig: its cavernous interior is open and clutter-free yet baits, sinkers and leaders are never more than a step away.

floor width. For freedrifting, he takes the seats out of the boat so there is nothing but open fishing room inside. Stationed at various points around the inside perimeter of the boat were several aluminum bait boxes filled with pre-cut clusters of beautiful eggs. Leader rolls were also located throughout the boat, so when we broke off, there were always fresh rigs close at hand. Holt also had several rods near the stern of the big boat that were completely rigged, if we broke everything off on a snag (leader, hook and sinker), we'd simply trade that rod for a "fresh" one. Sinkers were always handy as well so it was a snap to change weights when we had to. Being able to easily change your sinkers to match the water you're fishing is a subtle but extremely key element to successful side-drifting.

Putting it all together: Start with a solid foundation of fundamentals, throw in some practice, learn a few tricks and you'll soon be involved with more scenes like this one—a big fish in the net.

Everything about Holt's boat was geared for minimal downtime and there's a good lesson to be learned there: by being prepared and having all your gear dialed-in ahead of time, you'll spend more time fishing.

The Creature-of-Habit Syndrome

Kevin Brock, an especially successful guide in Northern California and routinely one of the top rods on the Smith River during steelhead season, attributes much of his success to the wholesale avoidance of the "Creature of Habit Syndrome."

He says that anglers have a tendency to do the same thing day in and day out, regardless of water and weather conditions. Good steelheaders, Brock notes, have to be open-minded and confident enough to break old habits and to adapt to ever-changing circumstances.

To accomplish this, Brock keeps a journal of how a river fishes under all conditions. He says that a certain spot may be perfect at mid-range flows but isn't worth a cast when the water's up or low. Some fruitful nooks and crannies may only materialize during peak flows, while others are ideal only when the water's down. By paying attention to all moods of a river, Brock can spend his time fishing the most productive lies without wasting time in spots that don't fish well in a given flow.

8
CHAPTER

GUIDE PROFILES

Kevin Brock

Home Rivers: Smith, Feather & Sacramento.

Main Techniques: Side-gliding, boondogging.

Outfit: G. Loomis HSR 930S (GL3) with Penn Slammer reel spooled with 12-pound PLine high-vis blue.

Tips from a Pro: There's a lot of debate out there regarding hook color and the effect it has on steelhead. Here's Brock's take…

"The fish don't care what color your hook is," he says. "But, I will tell you this: For side-gliding, I usually run No. 4 Gamakatsu octopus hooks and will always lean towards the black finish over the red ones if I have a choice. You'd think that they would be the same hook, but the black ones must be made from a different metal or something because they are stronger and stay sharper longer."

Kevin Brock.

Brock, somewhat of a hook junkie also offered up these tidbits:

"When the water gets low and clear, I switch to No. 4 Daiichi hooks as they are a half-size smaller than Gamakatsu's No. 4 and snag less," he says. "When I'm fishing low water on rivers with lots of pressure and smaller fish, I'll go even smaller and run a No. 8 Gami with a tiny piece of bait and small Quickie for flotation."

Contact: Telephone: (800) 995-5543; www.fishkevinbrock.com

Brett Brown

Home Rivers: Cowlitz, Green and Skykomish

Main Techniques: Freedrifting.

Outfit: G. Loomis STR 1141S rod with a Shimano Symetre or Sedona 2500 reel and 12-pound yellow Izorline.

Tips from a Pro: Drop into a tackle store and you'll be amazed at all the different colors, shapes and sizes of drift bobbers. Rather than being overwhelmed by the choices, Brown tries to keep it simple.

"I use mostly Corkies in the No. 14 size when the water's clear and No. 10 when it's up," he says. "As far as color goes, rocket red seems to be the ticket and that's what I use 99 percent of the time. Sometimes, I'll throw some rainbow-colored ones on for contrast in dirty water,

Brett Brown.

though. At first light, I like to use the glow-in-the-dark finish and I'll back away from any bobbers at all when the bite gets tough."

Brown's not a big fan of spinning drift bobbers in most cases, but he says they do have their moments.

"I don't like the spinning variety much because of the twist factor," he says. "But there are times when I'm flogging (see Chapter 7) a deep hole and need a little more flash and color. That's when I bust out the Spin-N-Glos or Spinning and Flashing Cheaters."

Contact: Telephone (877) 534-7466; www.alaskakingsalmon.com.

Ron DeNardi

Home Rivers: Chetco, Smith and Klamath

Main Technique: Side-gliding/freedrifting hybrid.

Outfit: Shimano CSS86M2 rod with a Shimano 2500 Stradic reel.

Tips from a Pro: When you guide fishing trips for over 30 years, you learn lots of tricks out on the river but DeNardi still believes that the

Justin Kelly and Ron DeNardi display a typical winter steelhead on Oregon's Chetco River.

real keys to success are making good casts, maximizing your time on the water and fishing hard.

"When you're setting up for a drift, don't be in a hurry," he says. "Take an extra second to relax and then make your cast count. And if you do mess up your cast, don't waste any more time reeling in and re-throwing. Make your cast and live with it as long as it gets down to the bottom."

DeNardi also says that you have to stay focused and keep working hard—even when the chips are down.

"You've really got to fish until the end," he says. "The very last cast may be the one that gets you your fish."

Contact: Telephone (530) 340-1345.

Justin Gyger & Gill McKean

Home Rivers: Skeena, Nass and Kitimat

Main Technique: Side-drifting with floats.

Outfit: Shimano CVC-L106M-2 casting rod with a Calcutta 250 levelwind reel spooled with 30-pound Power Pro braid.

Tips from a Pro: In some waters, securing enough eggs for an entire steelhead season can be a chore. In British Columbia, McKean and Gyger are staunch supporters of catch and release (even with king salmon), so fresh roe isn't easy to come by. In years past, that was a big issue for the pair but they have recently found a solution:

Gill McKean holds the beauty while Justin Gyger holds the rod.

"We've been making egg bags (spawn sacks) out of Pautzke's single Balls 'O Fire eggs straight out of the jar," says Gyger. "Those cured eggs don't wash out nearly as quickly as regular roe does and steelhead really seem to like them."

Depending on the size cluster they need, Gyger and McKean will fill their mesh bags with anywhere from 3 to 8 eggs. When they're side-drifting conventionally, the pair will add a small foam BFD to the bag to give it buoyancy. If they're float fishing, however, they'll tie their spawn sacks up with out any flotation.

On a Skeena River tributary in the spring of 2004, we watched Gyger land a 22-pound wild buck on a "Bag O' Fire" one day and hook about a dozen fish to 17 pounds the next— so the stuff obviously works!

Contact: Telephone (866) 578-8552; www.westcoastfishing.ca

Clancy Holt

Home Rivers: Cowlitz, Chehalis, Lewis and Columbia.

Main Technique: Freedrifting (he was one of the inventors!).

Outfit: G. Loomis STR1141 GLX spinning rod with a Shimano Stradic reel in the 2500 size spooled with 8- or 10-pound Ande line.

Clancy Holt.

Tips from a Pro: Every time the Godfather of Guides speaks, you can learn a lot. Here's what we picked up from Holt regarding hooks and sinker selection:

When deciding to use a double-hook tandem rig or a single, Holt says you have to look at the water conditions. Use a double setup when the water has some color to it and drop to a single when the water's clear and/or getting pressured. The two-hook deal can be a little intimidating when the fish can see well or are a little jittery, he says.

When freedrifting, Holt's a big fan of pencil lead because it gets down to the bottom well. In spots with lots of big boulders or other underwater structure, he switches to Slinkies because they are less apt to snag.

Contact: Telephone (800) 871-9549; www.clancysfishing.com

John Klar

Home Rivers: Smith, Eel, Mattole, Klamath and Mad.

Main Technique: Side gliding, boondogging.

Outfit: G. Loomis HSR 930S rod and Shimano Sustain 2500 spooled with 12-pound light blue Izorline.

Tips from a Pro: Because beginning side-drifters often ask about proper timing of the hookset, we asked Klar to shed some light on the subject.

"You want to set as soon as the bite is detected," he says. "Usually, by the time you feel the bite and realize what's happening, the fish has had your bait for a while.

Okay, so you're about to set the hook, but how hard?

John Klar.

"When you get bit, set the hook hard," he says. "It's rare that you'll break off on the set—if you do, I'll give you a pat on the back."

Contact: Telephone (707) 442-1867; www.johnklar.com

Khevin Mellegers

Home Rivers: Chetco, Klamath, Trinity and Smith.

Khevin Mellegers.

Main Techniques: Side-gliding.

Outfit: G. Loomis HSR930 spinning rod with a Stradic 2500 reel loaded 12-pound Suffix DNA yellow line.

Tips from a Pro: When it comes to casting order in a drift boat, there are several trains of thought. Some say it's best to have the angler in the left-seat cast first on

left side spots and then the right guy makes the first toss on right-side drifts. Mellegers makes a strong case for doing it the other way around ('goofyfoot'):

"If we're fishing to the left, I'll have the guy on the right go first," he says. "The left guy can easily point his rod down and out of the way while the other makes his cast. Then, the right-side guy can hold his rod low and pointed downstream while his partner makes his cast. The real advantage of doing it this way, though, is all about cast placement. The right side goes and then the left casts just a teeny skosh upriver. If the guy on the left goes first, the other fisherman is going to have to cast a little downstream of him and that means you'll get more tangles and not as good a drift."

Contact: Telephone (707) 826-7201; www.fishpills.com

About the Authors

J.D. Richey

J.D. Richey is a successful sportfishing guide who specializes in steelhead and salmon fishing in Northern California and Alaska. A well-known freelance outdoor writer and columnist, he has contributed thousands of articles to several national and regional publications such as *Field & Stream, Salmon Trout Steelheader, Fish Alaska* and *Western Outdoors* since 1990.

Contact: Telephone (916) 388-1956; www.thesportfisher.com

Authors Fred Contaoi (left) and JD Richey.

Fred Contaoi

Fred has been an ever-present figure in the fishing business for the past 20 years. He has fished, guided and worked in the fishing business in 30+ countries. His good nature has allowed him to fish all over the world and share his knowledge of everything from flyfishing to designing equipment. Fred is currently the Vice-President of the Lure Manufacturing Business of RiverzseaUSA. Yes, ladies, he is still single at the publishing of this book.

Contact: Telephone (209) 482-5652; www.westernguides.com

MORE GREAT FISHING INFORMATION!

COLOR GUIDE TO STEELHEAD DRIFT FISHING
Bill Herzog

Each year nearly 1,000,000 steelhead are hooked in North America and the great majority of these fish are hooked using drift fishing techniques. This lavishly illustrated, all-color guide is the "bible" if you want to get in on the action. Written by one of America's greatest drift fishermen, you will learn the techniques that can guarantee your entry into the 10% of the anglers who hook 90% of the steelhead. This is a heavy-duty grad

SB: $16.95

ISBN: 1-878175-59-9
UPC: 0-66066-00150-4

EGG CURES: PROVEN RECIPES & TECHNIQUES
Scott Haugen

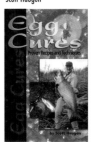

Of all the natural baits, many consider eggs to be the best. Before this book, you'd have an easier time getting the secret recipe for Coca-Cola than getting a fisherman to part with his personal egg cure. But now, Scott Haugen has done it for you, he went to the experts—fishermen and fishing guides—to get their favorite egg cures and fishing techniques, plus their secret tricks and tips. The result is this book. These 28 recipes come from anglers who catch fish—read this book and you will too. Guaranteed! 5 1/2 x 8 1/2 inches, 90 pages.

SB: $15.00

ISBN: 1-57188-238-3
UPC: 0-66066-00492-5

SUMMER STEELHEAD FISHING TECHNIQUES
Scott Haugen

Scott Haugen is quickly becoming known for his fact-filled, full-color fishing books. This time Haugen explores summer steelhead, including: understanding summer steelhead; reading water; bank, drift, and sight fishing; jigs, plugs, lures, dragging flies, and bait; fishing high, turbid waters; tying your own leaders; egg cures; gathering bait; do-it-your-self sinkers; hatchery and recycling programs; mounting your catch; cleaning and preparation; smoking your catch; and more. 6 x 9 inches, 135 pages.

SB: $15.95

ISBN: 1-57188-295-2
UPC: 0-81127-00125-5

STEELHEAD & SALMON DRIFT-FISHING TECHNIQUES
Timothy Kusherets

This comprehensive book goes way beyond the basics of drift-fishing techniques to include marine biology, ichthyology, meteorology, and physics as they apply to fish and fishing. Kusherets covers: species identification and anatomy; gear; set-ups; reading water; different drifting styles and techniques; understanding fish; spotting fish; troubleshooting; using the Internet; filleting your catch; extensive glossary; and more. The unique book will bring more fish to your line. 6 x 9 inches, 96 pages.

SB: $16.95

ISBN: 1-57188-300-2
UPC: 0-81127-00134-7

STEELHEAD DRIFT FISHING
with Bill Herzog and Nick Amato

Bill Herzog and Nick Amato will show you how to catch one of the world's favorite game fish. Not one, but two native winter steelhead pushing the 20-pound mark are hooked and released!

This tape will teach you everything you need to know to experience the thrill of hooking giant sea-run rainbow trout.

Subjects covered include: Seasons, range and types; reading water and decoding rivers; terminal gear and rigging; techniques for steelhead drift fishing; natural baits; and the tools—rods, reels, lines and other personal gear. 60 minutes.

DVD: $25.00

ISBN: 1-57188-335-5
UPC: 0-81127-00169-9

VIDEO: $25.00

ISBN: 1-57188-228-6
UPC: 0-0-66066-00482-6

FLOAT FISHING FOR STEELHEAD
with Nick, Rob, and Matt

Float-fishing for steelhead is very productive. It's the easiest and most effective way to hook steelhead. Nick Amato, Rob Crandall, and Canadian float-fishing expert Matt Guiguet, share the secrets for successful float-fishing. They cover: Rigging floats, jigs, and gear; fishing techniques and tips; equipment; reading water; and more. If you are looking to hook more steelhead, look no further. 60 minutes.

DVD: $25.00

ISBN: 1-57188-331-2
UPC: 0-81127-00168-2

VIDEO: $25.00

ISBN: 1-57188-249-9
UPC: 0-66066-00502-1